ME AND MY
WORLD

Help your child learn about these concepts:

- ⭐ *first and last names, address, telephone number, age, birthdate*
- ⭐ *home and family*
- ⭐ *the five senses: sight, hearing, smell, taste, touch*
- ⭐ *parts of the body; height; weight; and clothing*
- ⭐ *friends and feelings*
- ⭐ *school and neighborhood*
- ⭐ *favorite things and things he or she can do*
- ⭐ *day, night, and the seasons*

2

About Me and My World

Like most young children, kindergartners are curious and fascinated by the world around them. But how does their understanding of their environment evolve?

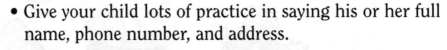

- Children first like to learn about themselves—how their names look in print, their age, their bodies, what they did when they were babies, their favorite things, and so on.

- Next, children learn about their primary environment—home and family—including family activities and traditions.

- As their horizons broaden, kindergartners become aware of areas beyond their own home—their neighborhood, their school, and aspects of the environment around them such as day and night, weather and the seasons.

- Soon their interest in people beyond their own family members grows—friends, teachers, neighbors, and workers in the community.

Experiences Are Key

Young children learn about the world through their senses: by seeing, hearing, smelling, tasting, and touching. All of these experiences help them develop a sense of self, a sense of family, and a sense of community.

There are many ways to help your child acquire the self-knowledge he or she needs to be ready for the learning that comes in school:

- Give your child lots of practice in saying his or her full name, phone number, and address.

- Talk about favorite family activities and traditions, and involve your child in planning special celebrations. Share stories, songs, foods, and other items that reflect your family's culture.

- Take your child to places in the neighborhood that you routinely visit: grocery store, gas station, bank, post office, library, park, and so on. Also, take nature walks and trips to places such as: a zoo, science museum, farm, beach, aquarium, botanical garden, and duck pond.

- Talk about what the weather is like and how the weather looks or feels. Make a chart to keep track of the weather, or create a seasonal collage.

- Keep a diary of your child's daily special events, and place papers and other important items in a "memory box." Create an "I Can Do It" wall chart to record new accomplishments, and make a book of "my favorite things." Activities such as these help build a positive sense of self—one of the most important ways you can prepare your child for success in life.

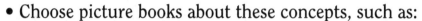

- Choose picture books about these concepts, such as:

- *Annabelle Swift, Kindergartner* by Amy Schwartz
- *Chicken Soup With Rice* by Maurice Sendak
- *Chrysanthemum* by Kevin Henkes
- *Do You Know What I'll Do?* by Charlotte Zolotow
- *Franklin's Neighborhood* by Paulette Bougeois and Brenda Clark
- *Here Are My Hands* by Bill Martin, Jr., and John Archambault

- *I Am Me* by Karla Kuskin
- *I'm Growing* by Aliki
- *Me and My Family Tree* by Joan Sweeney
- *My Favorite Time of Year* by Susan Pearson
- *My Five Senses* by Aliki
- *Will I Have a Friend?* by Miriam Cohen

The material in this book is based on tried-and-true strategies that teachers use throughout this country. The Parents Magazine Tips and Hands-On Activities will help you incorporate concept learning in a variety of activities that you and your child normally do throughout the day… and they'll help you make learning more fun! Remember that the ultimate goal of any instruction is not to teach isolated skills, but to impart strategies that children can use to learn throughout their lives.

Internet Resources for Parents

For articles and information about early learning and the stages of development of young children, check out these internet resources:

- Parents Magazine   http://www.parents.com

- Kid Source Online   http://www.kidsource.com

- Teaching Strategies, Inc.   http://www.teachingstrategies.com

- Learning Network Parent Channel   http://www.familyeducation.com

My Name

What is your name? How do you spell it? Circle the letters in your first name.

Parents MAGAZINE **TIP**

Give your child many chances to practice printing his or her own name. Print your child's name in large letters on a piece of paper. (Begin with first name; then work on last name.) Talk about how you form the letters as you write them. Have your child copy his or her name, make a name card for the table, and label belongings.

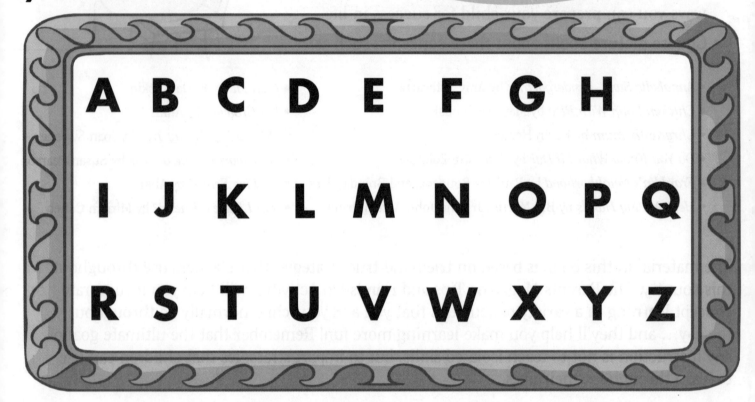

A B C D E F G H
I J K L M N O P Q
R S T U V W X Y Z

Write your first and last names.

My name is _____

_____ .

Skills: Identify the letters in your name; write first and last names.

What do you look like?

Draw your face and hair to finish the picture.

Write a number to finish each sentence.

I have _____ 👃.   I have _____ 👄.

I have _____ 👁 s.   I have _____ 👂 s.

Skills: Complete a picture; recognize and count facial features; write numerals to tell how many.

Hands-On Activity

Stick Puppets
Have your child draw faces on white paper plates. He or she can draw faces of family members, friends, or made-up characters. Tape or glue each face onto a craft stick and encourage your child to play act using the stick puppets.

My Address

Where do you live?

Write your name and address on the ✉ .

Name _____

Street _____

City and State _____

Zip Code _____

Skill: Write address.

What does your home look like?
Color the picture that looks most like your home.

Write a number to finish each sentence.

My home has _____ s.

My home has _____ s.

My home has _____ s.

My home has _____ s.

Skills: Count items in your house; write numerals to complete a sentence.

Hands-On Activity

Count Around the House
Continue to count clocks, tables, sinks, mirrors, steps, lamps, and any other items your child suggests. Before counting, ask him or her to estimate, or guess, how many. After counting, compare the estimate with the actual count.

My Phone Number

Parents MAGAZINE **TIP** Teach your child your phone number and 911. List all important numbers by the phone, and let your child practice making calls. Discuss types of emergencies and what to do in case one occurs.

What is your phone number?
Color the phone and say
the numbers.
Then write your phone number.

My phone number is

_____

8   Skill: Write telephone number.

How old are you? Draw candles on the cake to show your age. Then color the picture.

I am _____ **years old.**

My birthday is on

_____ .

Hands-On Activity

Plan a Party
When your child's birthday is four or five weeks away, let him or her help plan the party. Discuss where the party will take place, invitations, special activities and games, food, decorations, favors, and other details. To encourage literacy skills, help your child make a list of friends to invite.

My Family

Parents MAGAZINE TIP Talk about different kinds of families—big and small. Explain that "family" usually means the people living with you in your home, but grandparents, aunts, uncles, and cousins who do not live in your house are part of your "extended" family. To promote literacy, help your child label the family members in the picture that he or she draws.

Who is in your family? Draw a picture.

There are _____ people in my family.

I have _____ sisters.   I have _____ brothers.

Skills: Recognize, draw, and count people in your family; write a numeral to complete a sentence.

Color the pictures of things you like to do with your family.

My favorite family holiday is

_____ •

My favorite family vacation was

_____ •

Skills: Recognize family activities; write about favorite family times.

Hands-On Activity

Family Times Album
Create a photo album of special family times, including birthdays, holidays, visits to relatives, and vacations. Talk with your child about each picture. Write what your child says on self-stick notes to create captions for the photos.

11

My Eyes

You use your eyes to see things.
Look at the things in the box.
Find and circle them in the big picture.

What do you like to see?

I like to see

Explain that when we use our eyes, we're using our sense of sight to help us see. Then tell your child that people usually have five senses in all—sight, hearing, smell, taste, and touch—that they use to learn about the world around them.

Skills: Understand that eyes are for seeing; find things in a picture.

Hands-On Activity

What's That Sound?
Play this game. Put a blindfold on your child's eyes and ask him or her to listen while you make a sound. Use common house sounds such as: an alarm clock, a tea kettle, a television, a radio, a whistle, running water, a hair dryer, a musical instrument, and a blender. Ask your child to try to guess what is making the sound.

You use your ears to hear things. Color all the things you can hear.

What do you like to hear?

I like to hear_____.

Skills: Understand that ears are for hearing; color things that make sounds.

13

My Nose

Parents MAGAZINE TIP Tell your child that when we eat and drink, our sense of smell works together with our sense of taste. When we can't smell, it's harder to tell what foods taste like. Also point out that the tiny little bumps on our tongues are called taste buds. Our tongues have four different kinds of taste buds: sweet, sour, salty, and bitter.

You smell things with your nose.

Circle the things you like to smell.

Put an X on the things you do not like to smell.

What do you like to smell?

I like to smell _____.

Skills: Understand that the nose is for smelling; distinguish between things with good and bad smells.

You taste things with your tongue.

Color the foods that taste sweet .

Color the foods that taste salty .

What do you like to taste?

I like to taste _____ .

Skills: Understand that the tongue is for tasting; distinguish between different kinds of tastes.

15

My Hands

You touch things with your hands.

Write an X on the things that feel hard.

Circle the things that feel soft.

What do you like to touch?

I like to touch _____ .

Explain to your child that just under the skin are nerves that send messages to the brain about the way things feel—hard, soft, smooth, bumpy, hot, or cold. Some places on the body, like fingertips, have many nerves, so they are very sensitive.

Skills: Understand that hands are for touching; distinguish between things that feel hard and things that feel soft.

My Hands and Feet
Help your child trace his or her hands and feet onto a piece of paper with a crayon. Then help him or her measure hand span and foot length. (Hand span is the distance between the little finger and the thumb.) Use a ruler to measure in inches.

What can you do with your feet?
Draw a line from each picture to the correct word.

 •

• **jump**

 •

• **kick**

 •

• **run**

 •

• **ride**

My Body

Trace along the dotted lines. Then write numbers to finish the sentences.

I have _____ fingers.

I have _____ arms.

I have _____ legs.

I have _____ toes.

I weigh _____ pounds.   I am _____ inches tall.

Skills: Trace an outline of the body; identify and count parts of the body; know height and weight.

Color the 👕 🩳 **and** 👟 **to look like your favorites. Circle the other clothes you would like to wear.**

Skills: Color articles of clothing; identify favorite clothing.

My Friends

Draw pictures of two of your friends. Write their names.

Finish the sentence.

My friends and I like to _____

_____.

Skills: Draw pictures of friends; write friends' names; identify interests.

How would you feel?
Color the 😊 or ☹.

Hands-On Activity

Make a Mask
Have your child act out different feelings—happy, sad, scared, angry, surprised. Take turns pantomiming and guessing each other's feelings. Then, help your child use paper plates, pieces of construction paper, pom-poms, scraps of fabric, cotton balls, pipe cleaners, and markers to make masks for different feelings.

Skills: Recognize examples of happy and sad; identify feelings in various situations.

My School

Parents MAGAZINE **TIP**

After school starts, talk about your child's day when he or she gets home. Don't force conversation; just ask a few questions that might encourage dialogue. For example: What did you do at recess? What story did your teacher read today?

How do you get to school?

Color the correct picture.

Circle the things you do in school.

Skills: Identify how you get to school; identify activities that are done in school.

What does your neighborhood look like?
Color the picture that looks most like your
neighborhood.

Hands-On Activity

Build a Neighborhood
Help your child build a pretend neighborhood. Use cardboard boxes for
stores, houses, a bank, a post office, a grocery store, a school, a library,
a toy store, and a fire station. Color the boxes and glue on paper
doors and windows.

Skill: Identify what your neighborhood looks like.

23

My Favorite Foods

Parents MAGAZINE TIP Talk to your child about the importance of eating a variety of healthy foods. Include in your discussion foods from the basic food groups: fruits and vegetables; grains such as cereal, bread, and pasta; dairy products such as milk and yogurt; and protein such as fish and chicken. Tell your child that sweets should be only a small part of what they eat.

What do you like to eat? Draw your favorite foods.

24 Skill: Draw favorite foods.

My Favorite Things

What are your favorite things?
Write the word. Draw a picture.

My favorite color

My favorite toy

My favorite sport

My favorite book

Hands-On Activity

Make a Treasure Box
Have your child decorate a shoe box in which he or she can keep favorite things, such as small toys or figures, jewelry, rocks, shells, stickers, and other objects. Decorate the box with markers, glitter glue, and, if you wish, pictures cut from magazines.

Skill: Draw and write about favorite things.

What do you do every day?

Draw a line from each picture to the correct word.

• **eat**

• **dress**

• **wash**

• **play**

Parents
MAGAZINE
TIP

Talk about the importance of daily routines such as washing hands before meals, after playing outdoors, and after using the toilet; taking a bath; and brushing teeth after meals and before bedtime.

Skills: Recognize activities that are part of one's daily routine; match pictures to words.

 **Keep a Journal**

Help your child keep a daily journal. Make a book with blank pages, or buy a notebook and have your child decorate the cover. Ask your child to tell you about important things that happened each day at home or in school. Write what your child dictates and encourage him or her to illustrate the entries.

What do you do at night? In each row, write 1, 2, and 3 to show what you do first, next, and last.

Skill: Identify first, next, and last in a sequence of events.

My Winter

 **Parents** MAGAZINE **TIP** Discuss seasons with your child. Talk about the fact that some places stay warm all year, some places stay cold most of the year, and in other places the temperature changes. Talk about how the weather changes where you live and what it is like from season to season. Compare the seasons as you *go* through pages 28 to 29.

What is wrong with this winter picture? Write an X on the things that do not belong.

What do you like to do in the winter?

In winter I like to _____ .

Skills: Identify items that do not belong in a winter scene; write about a favorite winter activity.

What do you need in the summer? Color the ☀ **next to each thing you might need.**

What do you like to do in the summer?

In summer I like to _____ .

Skills: Identify clothing and items used in summer; write about a favorite summer activity.

Hands-On Activity

Make a List
Help your child make a list of things he or she would like to do in the summer, including visits to special places, family trips, and activities unique to summer. Encourage your child to use "invented spelling" (the way he/she hears the word) to write the list. You can write the "real" spelling next to each word.

When I Was Little

TIP

At this age, your child will love hearing your memories of when he or she was a baby and toddler. Recall an event and tell about it, share photos, and encourage your child to ask for more details. Help him or her complete the sentences at the bottom of pages 30 and 31.

What did you do when you were little?
Write 1, 2, or 3 in each box to tell how old you were.

When I was little I liked to

_____

_____.

Skill: Identify and tell about past events in one's life.

What does each grown-up need? Draw lines to match the workers to the things that belong to them.

When I grow up, I want to be

_____ •

Skills: Match workers and their tools; identify what you want to be when you grow up.

Hands-On Activity

Act It Out!
Take turns pantomiming the actions of different workers and guessing their occupations. You can also set up a grocery store, doctor's office, post office, restaurant, or other pretend place. Gather props and take turns being the customer, patient, owner, and so on.

31

Things I Can Do

 **TIP** Helping to develop a positive sense of self is one of the most important ways you can help your child succeed in school and in life! Talk about all of the things he or she can do and all the things that make him or her special. Help your child complete the bottom of the page.

Write a ✔ in each box next to the things you can do.

I can. . .

☐ **dress myself**

☐ **ride a bike**

☐ **write my name**

☐ **tie my shoes**

☐ **play ball**

Write more things you can do. I can also. . .

_____

_____

SOUNDS AND

Teach your child all about letters and sounds...

- *to recite the letters of the alphabet*
- *to identify capital and lowercase letters*
- *to match capital with lowercase letters*
- *to trace letters*
- *to recognize the sound of each letter*
- *to say the name of a picture and the letter it begins with*
- *to match pictures whose names begin with the same sound*
- *to recognize words that rhyme*

About Sounds and Letters

Before children can learn to read, they must learn the letters of the alphabet and the sounds they represent. What exactly does this entail? The answer is: many processes that we, as adults, often have forgotten over the years. For example:

- *Alphabet Recognition:* Being able to say the alphabet is not the same as "knowing" the letters. Can your child recognize all letters in both capital and lowercase forms? Can he or she distinguish among similar-looking letters—for example, the easily confused letters *E* and *F* and *b* and *d*?

- *Phonemic Awareness:* Understanding that a word is made up of individual sounds, or phonemes, and the ability to discriminate among these sounds is called *phonemic awareness.* It takes practice, for example, to hear the *sss* in the words *sit* and *sock* or to hear that *hat* and *mat* rhyme and understand that it's because they have the same ending sound. When children can connect the sound a letter makes to the printed letter, they are on the road to reading.

Teaching Sounds and Letters at Home

How can you help your child learn sounds and letters? Here are some ideas:

- Slowly say the sounds in words so your child can hear each one: *bbbaaattt*.

- Say a word, such as *ball*, and emphasize the beginning sound. Then ask your child to say another word that begins with the same sound.

- Play games with rhyming words. For example, say a word such as *cat* and ask your child to say a word that rhymes by changing the beginning sound: e.g., *bat*. Or, say a familiar nursery rhyme; along the way, leave out a rhyming word; then pause so your child can say it.

- Say a letter and ask your child to find it in a set of magnetic letters.

- Make clay *ABCs* to help teach letter shapes. Talk about how the letters are alike and how they are different.

Sounds and Letters Every Day

Help your child become aware of letters and their sounds by incorporating these activities into daily routines:

- Use the alphabet song (the alphabet sung to the tune of "Twinkle, Twinkle, Little Star") to familiarize your child with letter names and alphabetic sequence.

- Practice identifying letters—in books and magazines, on cereal boxes, and so on. Label objects around the house with words and underline the beginning letters.

- Read alphabet books and rhyming picture books, such as these:

- *A, B, See!* by Tana Hoban
- *A Big and Little Alphabet Book* by Liz Rosenberg
- *Alphabetics* by Sue MacDonald
- *Anno's Alphabet* by Mitsumaso Anno
- *Chicka Chicka Boom Boom* by Bill Martin, Jr., and J. Archambault
- *Hop on Pop* by Dr. Seuss

- *Is Your Mama a Llama?* by Deborah Guarino
- *It Begins With an A* by Stephanie Calmenson
- *Jamberry* by Bruce Degan
- *Sheep in a Jeep* by Nancy Shaw
- *Silly Sally* by Audrey Wood
- *The Hullabaloo ABC* by Beverly Cleary

The material in this book is based on tried-and-true strategies that teachers use throughout this country. The Parents Magazine Tips and Hands-On Activities will help you incorporate learning about sounds and letters into a variety of activities that you and your child normally do throughout the day…and they'll help you make learning more fun! Remember that the ultimate goal of any instruction is not to teach isolated skills, but to impart strategies that children can use to learn throughout their lives.

Internet Resources for Parents

For articles and information about early learning and the stages of development of young children, check out these internet resources:

- Parents Magazine   http://www.parents.com

- Kid Source Online   http://www.kidsource.com

- Teaching Strategies, Inc.   http://www.teachingstrategies.com

- Learning Network Parent Channel   http://www.familyeducation.com

I Know My ABCs!

Do you know the letters of the alphabet?
Point to each letter and say its name.
Then color the picture.

Parents MAGAZINE **TIP** Introduce letter names by singing the alphabet song. Sing slowly, pointing to each letter on the page as you sing. Remember, children can recite the alphabet before they can attach names to letter forms. Find out what your child already knows about letter recognition by seeing how many letters he or she can identify.

Skills: Recite the letters of the alphabet; identify letters.

Looking for Letters
Pick a letter of the day and look for it everywhere:
on clothing, on cereal boxes, on street signs, on
license plates, and on supermarket shelf labels. Cut out examples
of the letter from magazines and newspapers and
paste onto a card.

E F G H I J K
O P Q R S
W X Y Z

Skills: Recite the letters of the alphabet; identify letters.

Alligator's Big Letters

 likes to print capital letters.

Circle the letter that is the same as the first one in each row.

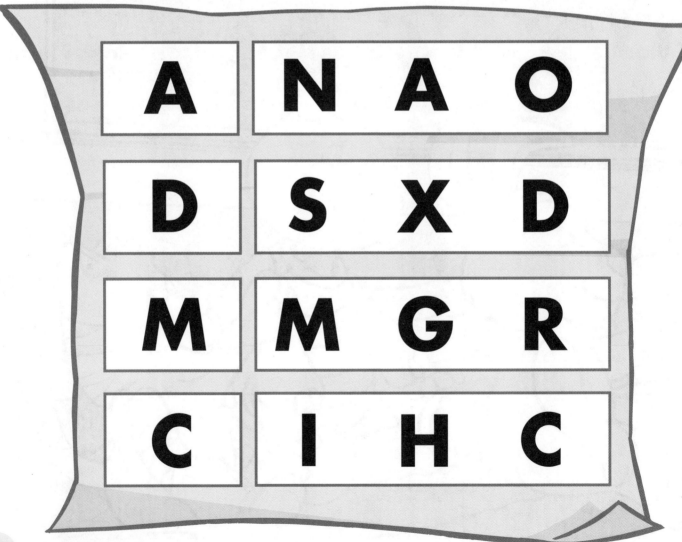

A	N A O
D	S X D
M	M G R
C	I H C

Skill: Identify matching capital letters.

Hands-On Activity — **Roll a Letter**
Make a giant alphabet cube by taking a square tissue box and covering each side with a paper letter. Take turns rolling the cube and naming the letter that is face up when the cube lands.

Look at what built with blocks!

Color the 2 blocks in each tower that have the same letter.

Tower 1: I P I F

Tower 2: K J J W

Tower 3: U T B U

Tower 4: V E S E

Skill: Identify capital letters that are the same.   39

Bear's Small Letters

Parents MAGAZINE TIP

At this age, it can be difficult for children to distinguish between letters of the alphabet. You can help by providing cut-out letters to touch, since the sense of touch is often keener than sight and sound in preschoolers. Cut out letters from sandpaper, felt, or another material. Encourage your child to handle each letter.

 likes to print lowercase letters at the playground.

Write an X on the letter that is different in each tower.

Skill: Identify lowercase letters that are different.

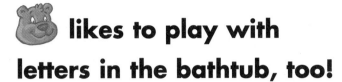 likes to play with letters in the bathtub, too!

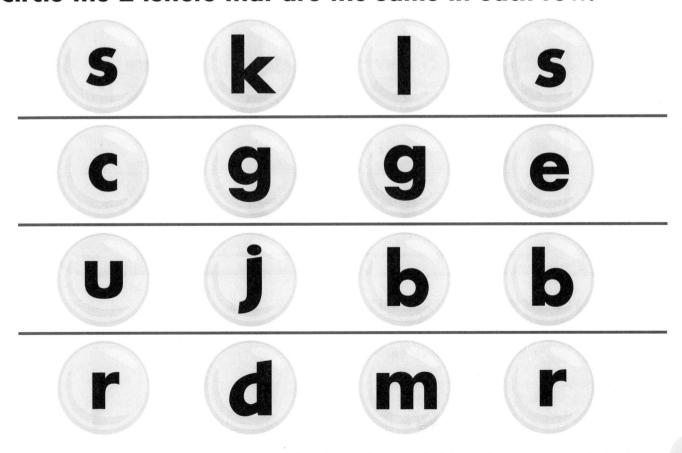

Circle the 2 letters that are the same in each row.

s k l s

c g g e

u j b b

r d m r

Skill: Identify matching lowercase letters.

Cat in the Kitchen

 is learning letters in the kitchen.
She has capital letters and lowercase letters.
Circle the lowercase letter in each row that
matches the capital letter.

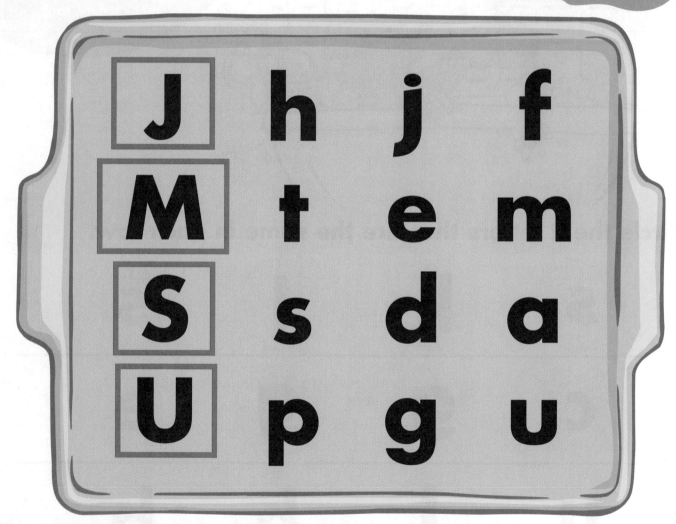

J	h	j	f
M	t	e	m
S	s	d	a
U	p	g	u

Skill: Match capital and lowercase letters.

left these letters for you!

Circle the lowercase letter in each row that matches the capital letter.

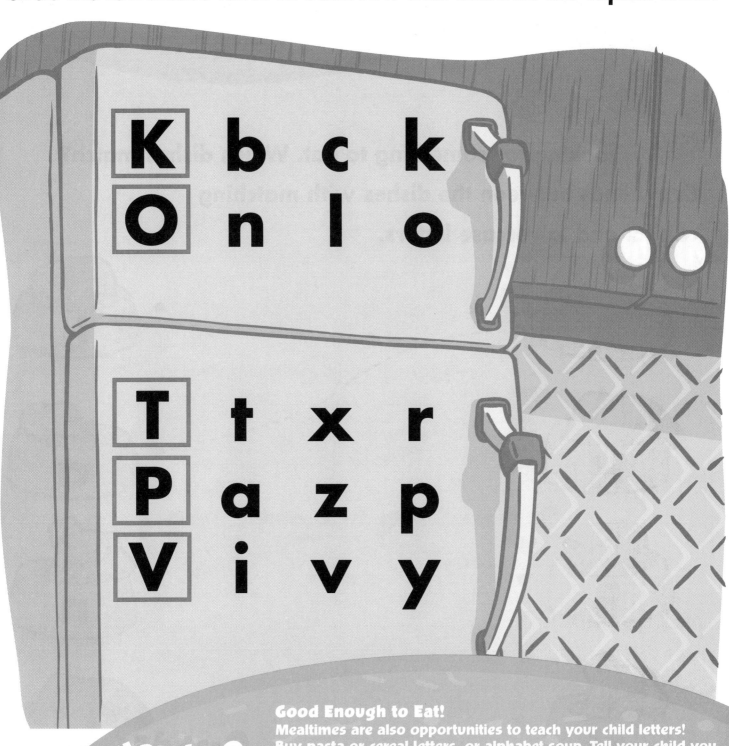

K   b   c   k

O   n   l   o

T   t   x   r

P   a   z   p

V   i   v   y

Hands-On Activity

Good Enough to Eat!
Mealtimes are also opportunities to teach your child letters! Buy pasta or cereal letters, or alphabet soup. Tell your child you are hungry for an A, would like to taste a T, and so on. You can also form pancake batter into letters, using a turkey baster.

Skill: Match capital and lowercase letters.

43

Dishes for Dogs

 is looking for something to eat. Which dishes match? Draw lines between the dishes with matching capital and lowercase letters.

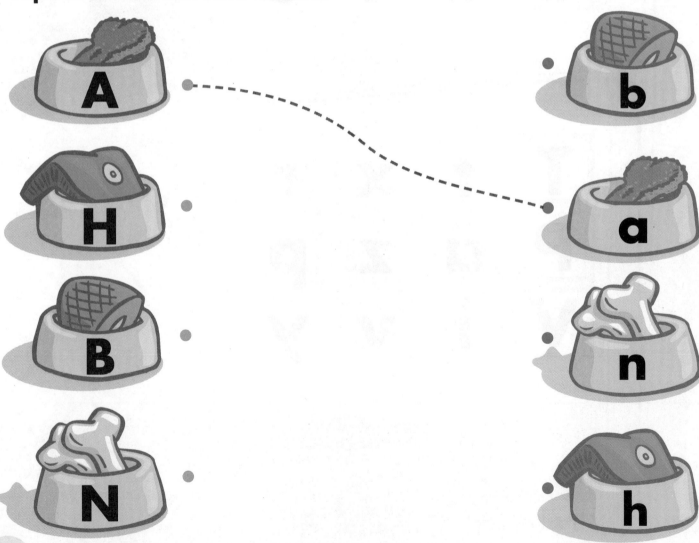

Skill: Match capital and lowercase letters.

Help these s find the right dishes!

Draw lines between the matching capital and lowercase letters.

Here's a game to play.
Try to be the first  to get to the cheese!

Parents MAGAZINE **TIP** To play the game on these pages, you will need a coin and two playing pieces (such as buttons of different colors). Take turns with your child. Flip the coin. If it lands on heads, move one space. If it lands on tails, move two spaces. Say the name of the letter you land on. (Help your child identify the letter as needed.) Race to the cheese!

46 **Skill:** Identify the letters of the alphabet.

Walk the Alphabet

Make an alphabet path by writing the letters A to Z on the sidewalk in chalk. Have your child "walk" the alphabet, saying aloud each letter name as he or she steps on it.

Hands-On Activity

M N O P Q R S T U V W X Y Z

Trace each letter and say its name.

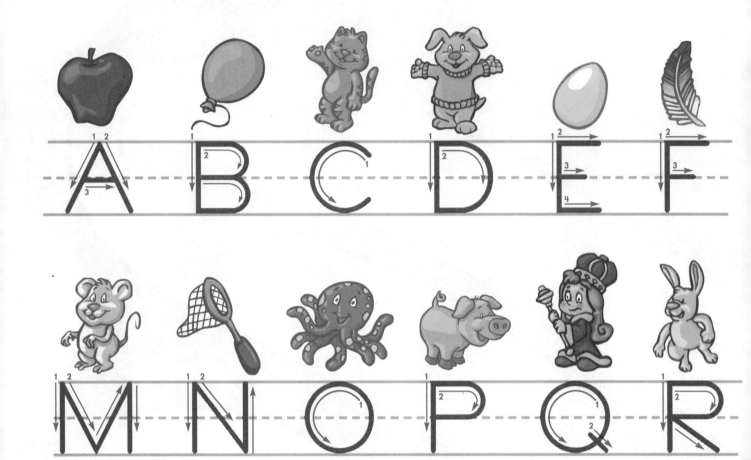

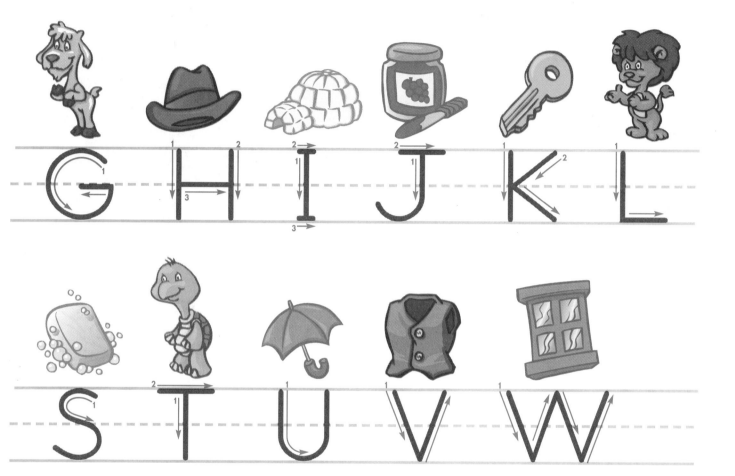

G H I J K L

S T U V W

X Y Z

Skill: Trace capital letters A to Z.

Bear's Bike

 and  begin with the sound of **b**.
Say the name of each picture.
Listen to the beginning sound.

Bear

bike

Color the pictures that start
with the sound of **b**.

Parents MAGAZINE **TIP** After children have learned letter names and forms, the next step is to learn to associate speech sounds with written letters. When teaching the match between the printed letter and the spoken sound, focus on the sound first. For example, say: Bear begins with the sound of b--buh. Ask your child to say the sound at the beginning of bike (buh). Then, point to the letter that stands for buh. . . b.

Skills: Recognize the sound for /b/b;
identify picture names that start with /b/b.

50

and begin with the sound of m.

Say the name of each picture.
Listen to the beginning sound.

Mouse

motorcycle

Circle the pictures that start with the sound of m.

Hands-On Activity

A Letter a Day
Dedicate each day to a different letter. On B day, for example, find as many objects as you can that start with B. Also, plan activities associated with B words, such as eat bananas, play ball, and blow bubbles.

Skills: Recognize the sound for /m/m; identify picture names that start with /m/m.

Pig in School

Parents MAGAZINE TIP

Phonemic awareness is the ability to hear sounds in words. This skill is a prerequisite for learning to read. To help your child distinguish individual sounds, as you identify each picture, separate the beginning sound from the rest of the word. For example, say puh-uzzle or kuh-ars.

 likes to play with things that begin with the sound of **p**.

Listen for the beginning sound as you say the name of each picture.

Draw a line from Pig to the pictures that begin with the sound of **p**.

Skills: Recognize the sound for /p/p; identify picture names that start with /p/p.

wants to put things that begin with the sound of **t** in his tent.
Listen for the beginning sound as you say the name of each picture.
Color the things that belong in Tiger's tent.

Hands-On Activity

A Letter Book
Choose a letter and, together, look through magazines and find pictures of things whose names begin with that letter. Cut out each picture and glue it on a sheet of paper. Write the name of the picture underneath. Staple the pages together to make a book your child can read.

Skills: Recognize the sound for /t/t; Identify names that start with /t/t.

Seal's Sounds

 likes to balance things that begin with the same sound.

Say the name of the picture in the box.

Listen for the sound at the beginning of the name.

Circle the 2 pictures in each row whose names begin with the same sound.

Skill: Match pictures whose names begin with the same sound.

Say the name of each picture.
Listen to the beginning sound.
Draw a line to match the
pictures whose names begin
with the same sound.

Hands-On Activity

Match that Sound
Say a list of words that begin with the same sound, for example: **Mommy, mouse, milk.** Ask your child to tell you another word that that begins with the same sound.

Skill: Match pictures whose names begin with the same sound.

Raccoon's Race

 Learning the relationship between how letters look and how they sound is an important pre-reading skill because knowing the sound/symbol match will make it possible to figure out unknown words later on. Letter cards that involve objects beginning with a particular letter sound, such as the ones described in the Hands-On Activity on page 57, will help your child make these associations.

 is running in a race.

His 👕 should show the first letter of his name.

Circle the 👕 Raccoon should wear.

Then color the picture.

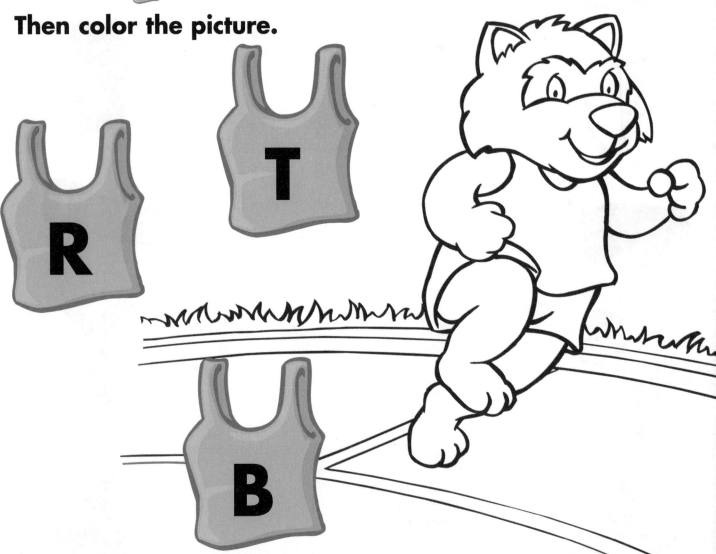

Skill: Associate the sound and symbol for the letter R.

These animals want to run in the race, too!

Say the name of each animal.

Draw a line to the 🎽 that the animal should wear.

D

F

H

B

Hands-On Activity

Make Letter Cards
Make letter cards that will help your child remember the shape of a letter and the sound the letter stands for. For example, glue on beads in the shape of a b for the letter b; paint a p for the letter p; make an m out of macaroni; cut out velvet in the shape of a v for the letter v; and glue on yarn in the shape of a y for the letter y.

Skill: Associate the sound and symbol for the letters B, D, F, and H.

 is sorting his toys by beginning sound.

He put his in the bin

with the letter **c**.

Help  sort these toys.

Say the name of each toy.

Draw a line to the bin with the correct beginning letter.

Parents MAGAZINE **TIP** If your child has difficulty hearing the beginning sound, say the word slowly, repeating the beginning sound. For example, for car, say **ccccar** (**kuh, kuh, kuh, car**), and have him or her repeat the word. Then say several additional words with the same beginning sound.

Skill: Associate the sound and symbol for the letters b, j, and y.

 forgot to put
these toys in bins.
Say the name of each toy.
Draw a line to the bin with
the correct beginning letter.

Skill: Associate the sound and symbol for the letters d, f, h, m, and r.

Cat's Rhymes

Parents MAGAZINE TIP An important part of phonemic awareness, rhyming focuses on words with ending sounds that match. Tell your child that rhyming words are words that sound the same at the end. Say mop and top, for example, and explain that they both end with **op**. Then show your child how to change the beginning sound to make another word that rhymes, such as hop.

 likes things that rhyme with his name.
Color all the pictures that rhyme with .

60 Skill: Recognize rhyming words.

likes things that rhyme with her name, too.
Draw a line from  to each picture name that rhymes.

Hands-On Activity

Rhyme Time
Play a rhyming game in which you say three words—such as hat, bug, cat—and have your child repeat the two that rhyme. For an added challenge, say aloud two rhyming words (such as hen and ten), and ask your child to suggest another word that rhymes.

Skill: Recognize rhyming words.

More Fun with Rhymes!

Say the names of the pictures in each box.

Circle the two pictures that rhyme.

Skill: Match rhyming pictures.

A B C D E

F G H I J

K L M N O

P Q R S T

U V W X Y

Z

Remove the page from the book and cut out the cards. The capital letters are on the red side and the lowercase letters are on the blue side. Have your child pick a letter, say its name, and then find the matching capital or lowercase letter.

Skill: Match capital and lowercase letters A to Z. 63

z y x w v
u t s r q
p o n m l
k j i h g
f e d c b
a

Skill: Match capital and lowercase letters A to Z.

Sticker Activity

Have your child identify the capital and lowercase letter on each sticker. Then help peel off each sticker and place it on an index card. Save the cards and use them with the stickers on other sticker page.

Aa	Bb	Cc	Dd	Ee
Ff	Gg	Hh	Ii	Jj
Kk	Ll	Mm	Nn	Oo
Pp	Qq	Rr	Ss	Tt
Uu	Vv	Ww	Xx	Yy
Zz	WoW	WoW	WoW	WoW

Sticker Activity

Have your child identify the picture on each sticker and say the sound and letter that begins each picture name. Then help to peel off each sticker and place it on an index card. Use these sticker cards in combination with the cards made from the stickers from the previous sticker page. Have your child match each picture card to the correct letter card.

BEGINNING

> Teach your child all about the relationship between letters and sounds...
>
> ⭐ *to recognize the sound of each letter*
>
> ⭐ *to identify the letter that stands for each sound*
>
> ⭐ *to write each letter of the alphabet*
>
> ⭐ *to recognize words that rhyme*

About Beginning Phonics

Phonics is the relationship between sounds and their spellings. Studies suggest that children exposed to phonics instruction early have a head start in learning to read and spell, because they learn—

- that each letter of the alphabet represents a sound.
- that words can be broken down into their sounds, or sounded out.
- that blending sounds together is the way we read.
- that breaking down words into their sounds is the way we spell.

Teaching Phonics At Home

Teaching phonics may be new to you. For example, you've probably never heard the term "phonemic awareness." Simply put, this is the understanding that a word is made up of separate sounds, or *phonemes*. In print, those sounds are represented by a letter between two slash marks: e.g., /b/ stands for *buh*, the sound of the letter *b*.

To provide practice in phonemic awareness:

- Use magnetic letters to build word families, such as *bat, cat, fat, hat, mat, sat,* and so on. Then, use the words to create rhymes or nonsense poems.

- Make up silly sentences in which the first letter of most words contains the same sound: *Farley Fox has four furry feet.*

- Slowly, say the sounds in a word so your child can hear each one: *hhhaaattt.* Place extra emphasis on sounds that may be difficult for your child to hear, such as short vowel sounds: *heeeeeen.*

- Say a word sound-by-sound and have your child put the sounds together to make the word: for example, *j-a-m.*

- Say a three-letter word, then change the first sound and ask your child which sound is different: e.g., *ten, men.* Repeat this activity for final sounds—e.g., *tag, tap*—and vowel sounds—*pan, pen.*

Becoming Aware of Words

It's easy to practice phonics skills with children—words are everywhere in daily life! Help them become aware of words and how to sound out what they see:

- Read signs together as you walk around the neighborhood.

- Read the labels on favorite snack-food containers.

- Choose movies at the video store and sound out words in the title.

- Most important of all, read to your child as often as possible. Find books that reinforce phonics skills, such as:

- *A Giraffe and a Half* by Shel Silverstein
- *All About Arthur* by Eric Carle
- *Chicka Chicka Boom Boom* by Bill Martin, Jr. and John Archambault
- *Eating Alphabet Soup* by Lois Ehlert

- *Hop on Pop* by Dr. Seuss
- *Is Your Mama a Llama?* by D. Guarino
- *Jesse Bear, What Will You Wear?* by Nancy White Carlstrom
- *Six Sick Sheep* by Joanna Cole and Stephanie Calmenson
- *Street Rhymes Around the World* by Jane Yolen

The material in this book is based on tried-and-true strategies that teachers use throughout this country. The Parents Magazine Tips and Hands-On Activities will help you incorporate phonics learning in a variety of activities that you and your child normally do throughout the day…and they'll help you make learning more fun! Remember that the ultimate goal of any instruction is not to teach isolated skills, but to impart strategies that children can use to learn throughout their lives.

Internet Resources for Parents

For articles and information about early learning and the stages of development of young children, check out these internet resources:

- Parents Magazine http://www.parents.com

- Kid Source Online http://www.kidsource.com

- Teaching Strategies, Inc. http://www.teachingstrategies.com

- Learning Network Parent Channel http://www.familyeducation.com

Bear's Birthday

begins with /b/. Today is Bear's birthday!
Color all the things that begin with b.

Bear likes to ride on this.
Trace b to finish
the word.

bike

68 **Skills:** Recognize the sound and symbol for /b/b; write the letter b.

 begins with /f/.
Follow her footprints.
Find and circle 4 things that begin with f.

Fox has four of them.
Trace f to finish the word.

feet

Hands-On Activity

Search for Sounds
Walk around your house with your child to see how many items you can find that begin with /f/. Label each item and together say its name aloud. Blend the letters of the word as you say it.

Horse Is Hungry

begins with /h/.

Horse is hungry! Help him find hay.

Follow the path of pictures that begin with h.

Parents MAGAZINE **TIP** As you point to each picture, show your child how to blend sounds into words. Say the sounds slowly, so your child can hear each one. Stretch out the word "hat," for example, and say, "hhhaaattt." Gesture with your hands from left to right to show when you move from one sound to the next. Blending will help your child learn how sounds go together to make words.

A horse has this.

Trace h to finish the word.

hoof

Skills: Recognize the sound and symbol for /h/h; write the letter h.

 begins with /m/.
Mouse has many mirrors.
Circle the ones that show
things that begin with **m**.

m

Trace _m_ to answer this riddle.

Who do I see in the mirror?

me

Skills: Recognize the sound and symbol for /m/m; write the letter m.

begins with /s/.

Silly Seal has fun in the sun.

Find and circle 6 pictures that begin with s.

What's high in the sky?

Trace s to finish the word.  sun

As you identify each picture, separate the beginning sound from the rest of the word. For example, you might say s·un or s·ocks. Segmenting words will help prepare your child to separate words into their sounds in order to spell them.

Skills: Recognize the sound and symbol for /s/s; write the letter s.

Hands-On Activity

Tick, Tock Goes the Clock
Say aloud a variety of words, many of which begin with t. Each time your child hears /t/, he or she must say, "Tick, tock." Record the number of times your child identifies t words in one minute.

 begins with /t/.

Let's go to Turtle's tea party.

Color all the pictures that begin with t.

A clock says this.

Trace t to finish the words.

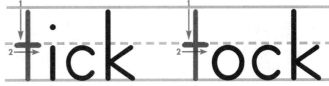

tick tock

Skills: Recognize the sound and symbol for /t/t; write the letter t.

Happy Cats

cat

Parents
MAGAZINE
TIP

Remind your child that he or she has been listening for sounds at the beginning of words: /b/ in ball, /m/ in mitt. Now he or she is going to listen for sounds in the middle of words. Have your child count the sounds in the word as you say /c/ - /a/ - /t/. Now say the word again, cccaaattt, and ask your child to listen for the sound in the middle of the word. Point to the letter in the cat's box as you say the sound together: /a/.

Say /a/ as in a c<u>a</u>t .

Now let's say each picture name.

Circle the if you hear /a/.

Put an X on the if you *do not* hear /a/.

Skills: Recognize the sound and symbol for short vowel /a/a.

Draw lines from the  to the picture names that rhyme.

You do this when you touch a cat's head. Trace *a* to finish the word.

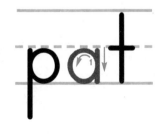

Skills: Identify rhyming words with short vowel /a/a; write the letter a.

Dinosaur's Diner

 **begins with /d/.**

Dinosaur's friends love dinner at the diner!

Circle all the things that begin with d.

You put dessert on this.

Trace d to finish the word.

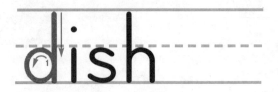

Parents
MAGAZINE
TIP

Children who are beginning to write may confuse b and d. One fun way to help is to turn the word into a drawing of a bed, like this: Tuck the letters b and d under a blanket at the beginning and end of the word.

76

Skills: Recognize the sound and symbol for /d/; write the letter d.

Hands-On Activity

Get to the Game
Set a destination, such as the table where your child's favorite game is displayed. Have your child stand a few feet away. Explain that for each word you say that begins with g your child may move one step forward. If a word does not begin with g, he or she must remain in place. Count how many steps it takes to "get to the game." Then play the game together.

begins with /g/.

Goat loves to play golf!

Draw lines from Goat to the things that begin with g.

It's the opposite of stop.

Trace g to finish the word.

Lion's Laundry

Parents MAGAZINE TIP

The letter l is often difficult for young children to pronounce. If your child is having a tough time with this letter, think of a few phrases such as lions like lollipops to say aloud for practice. First, say the phrase. Then, have your child repeat it. Show your child how to gently touch the front of the tongue behind the upper front teeth to make the sound. Exaggerate the movement and have fun!

begins with /l/. Lion has lots of laundry!
Circle the pictures that begin with *l*.

Lion likes to eat this. Trace *l* to finish the word.

Skills: Recognize the sound and symbol for /l/l; write the letter l.

 begins with /n/.

Nurse Nancy has a cold in her nose.

Help her find the doctor.

Draw a line through the maze.

Follow the pictures that begin with n.

It's the number after 8.

Trace n to finish the word.

 **9**

Skills: Recognize the sound and
symbol for /n/n; write the letter n.

Hands-On Activity

A Noodle Necklace
Show your child how to string noodles onto yarn to make a noodle necklace. As you string noodles, ask your child to name words that begin with n, like noodle.

The Very Best Hen

hen

Say /e/ as in h**e**n.

Now let's say each picture name.

Color the egg if you hear the /e/ sound.

Which hen has the most eggs with /e/?

Skills: Recognize the sound and symbol for short vowel /e/e.

Hands-On Activity

An "Egg" Hunt
Draw an *egg* on six separate index cards. Then write a word with short e inside each one: ten, men, hen, pen, let, jet. Hide the "eggs" around your house and have your child search for them. Each time he or she finds one, your child must read each word with /e/ as in *egg*.

Draw lines to match the picture names that rhyme.

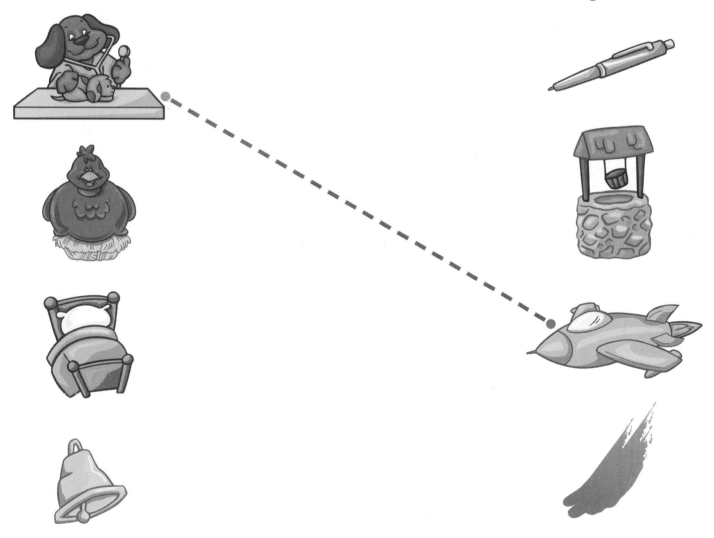

It's the opposite of dry.

Trace e to finish the word. wet

Skills: Identify rhyming words with short vowel /e/e; write the letter e.

81

Piggy's Pennies

Parents MAGAZINE TIP The letters b, d, and p are easily confused. Use your child's sense of touch to reinforce each letter's shape by having him or her trace each letter in salt or peanut butter that has been spread across a cookie sheet!

 begins with /p/.

Piggy has pennies. Help her buy things with

Draw lines to the things she will buy.

Piggy likes this sweet treat.

Trace p to finish the word. pie

Skills: Recognize the sound and symbol for /p/p; write the letter p.

begins with /w/.

Wolf has a wagon. Help him fill it.

Circle all the things that begin with w.

Humpty Dumpty sat on this!

Trace _w_ to finish the word.

wall

Hands-On Activity

Wooly Wormy Words

Cut pipe cleaners or string
into 1-inch strips to make wooly worms. Ask your child to glue 4
worms onto paper to form the letter w. Then, brainstorm a list of words
that begin with the letter. Each time you say a word, have your child trace
the wormy w with his or her fingers to reinforce the letter's shape.

fish

Say /i/ as in fish .

Now let's say each picture name.

Circle the if you hear /i/.

Put an X on the  if you do not hear /i/.

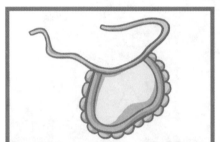

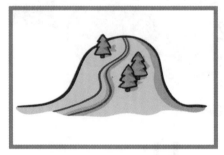

Draw lines to match the picture names that rhyme.

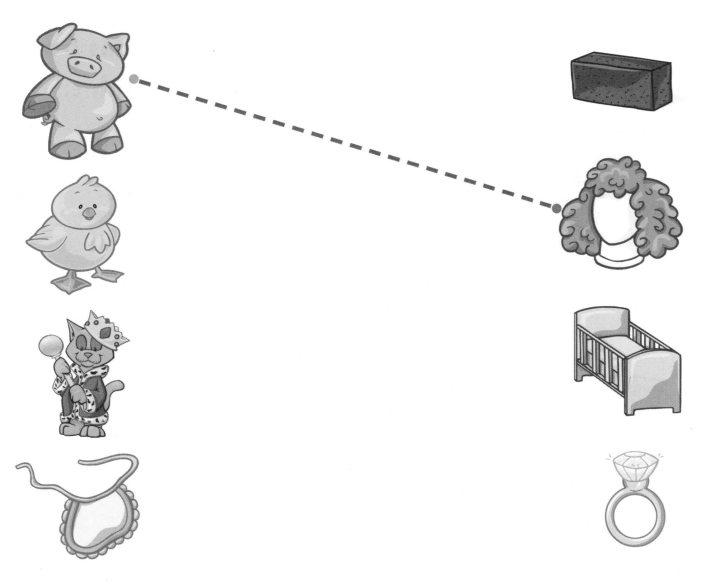

Jack and Jill went up it.

Trace _i_ to finish the word.

Cow Goes to Camp

Parents MAGAZINE **T I P** The letter c stands for more than one sound. When it comes before a, o, and u, it usually makes the /k/ sound as in cat, cot, and cut. When it comes before e, i, and y, it usually makes the /s/ sound as in cereal, circle, and cymbals. Review both sounds of c as you introduce new words to your child.

 begins with /c/.

Help Cow pack for camp. Draw lines from the  to the things that begin with c.

Cow must paddle to make it go. Trace c to finish the word.

canoe

Skills: Recognize the sound and symbol for /c/c; write the letter c.

begins with /j/.

Help take this to Jill's house.

Draw a line through the maze.

Follow the pictures that begin with *j*.

It is something you wear.

Trace *j* to finish the word.

2
1
j eans

Skills: Recognize the sound and
symbol for /j/j; write the letter j.

The King's Kite

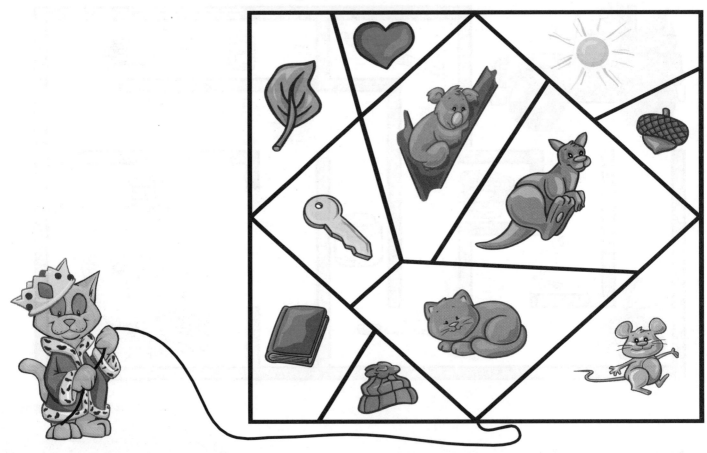 begins with /k/.

Help the 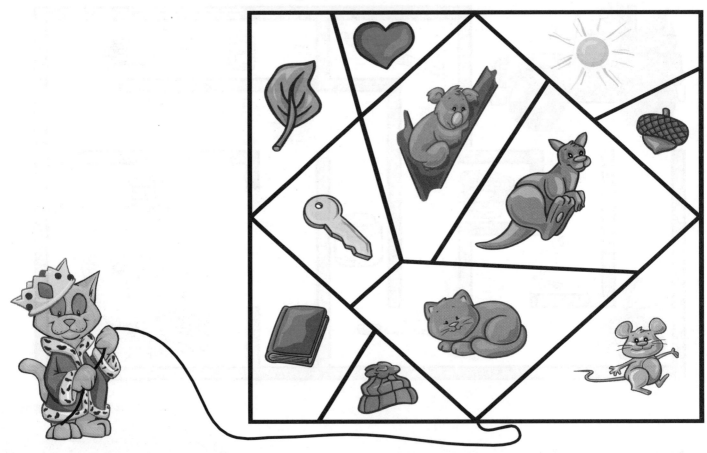 find his kite!

Color the spaces

if you hear the /k/ sound.

if you do not hear the /k/ sound.

It goes with a hug. Trace _k_ to finish the word.

Your child might have already noticed that the letter k sometimes makes the same sound as the letter c at the beginning of a word. This may create some slight confusion when your child begins to spell. In such instances, remembering what a word looks like can help your child use the right letter.

kiss

Skills: Recognize the sound and symbol for /k/k; write the letter k.

begins with /r/.

Help Rabbit's robot clean Rabbit's room.

Circle all the things on the floor that

begin with r.

You'll find it on the floor.

Trace r to finish the word.

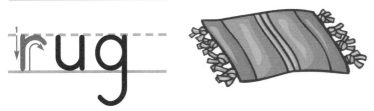

rug

Skills: Recognize the sound and
symbol for /r/r; write the letter r.

Hands-On Activity

A Rainbow of "R" Words
Brainstorm a list of words
whose names begin with r.
Write them in large, bold letters
on a sheet of paper. Then have
your child trace over the words,
using a different color of the
rainbow for each one.

89

A Jogging Frog

frog

Say /o/ as in frog .

Now let's say each picture name.

Color the 🪷 if you hear the /o/ sound.

Which frog can get across the pond?

Parents MAGAZINE TIP Listening for the same sound in a series of words is great practice for hearing short vowel sounds. Say box, clock, and shop, for example, and ask your child to identify the sound that is the same in each word. Repeat by saying other words with short vowel sounds until your child can identify each one.

Skills: Recognize the sound and symbol for short vowel /o/o.

Draw lines to match the picture names that rhyme.

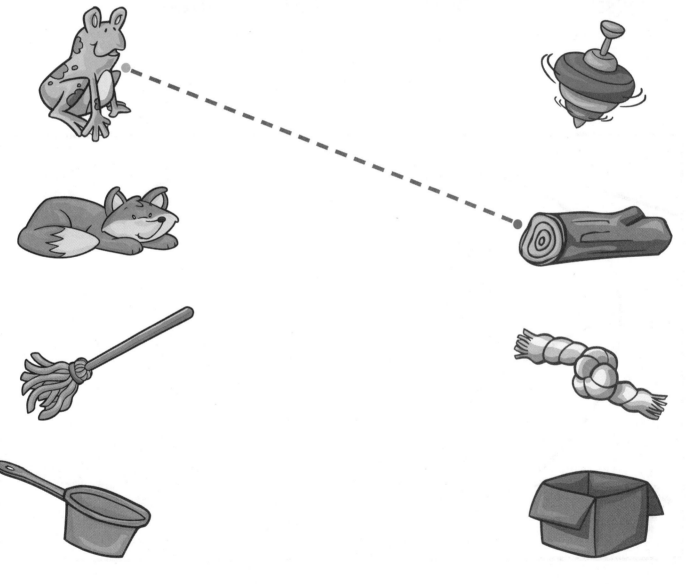

What do frogs do?

Trace _o_ to finish the word.   hop

Val's Valentine

Parents MAGAZINE **TIP**
The letters v and w are easily confused. Point out that the letter w looks like two letter v's put together. Practice forming the letters with your child.

 begins with /v/.

Find the hidden valentine.

Color the spaces 🖍 if you hear the /v/ sound.

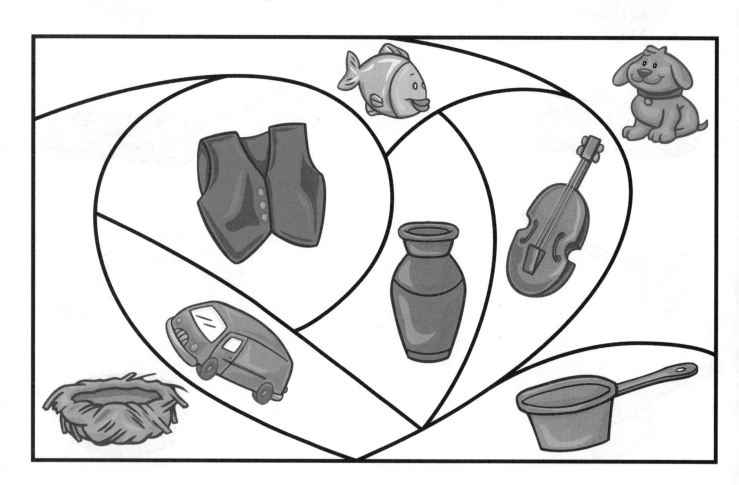

You put flowers in it.

Trace v to finish the word. **vase**

Skills: Recognize the sound and symbol for /v/v; write the letter v.

 begins with /y/.

Help Yak find his way to the zoo.

Draw a line through the maze.

Follow the pictures that begin with y.

Now the yak is in the zoo.

Trace y and z to finish the words.

yak   zoo

Skills: Recognize the sound and symbol for
/y/y and /z/z; write the letters y and z.

Hands-On Activity

Say "Yes" for Y
Say assorted words to
your child, including words
that begin with /y/. Have
your child say "Yes!" each
time he or she hears a
word that begins with y.

Lucky Ducks

d**u**ck

Parents MAGAZINE **TIP** Use picture clues to help your child remember short vowel sounds: apple for a; elephant for e; igloo for i; octopus for o; and umbrella for u.

Say /u/ as in d**u**ck .

Now let's say each picture name.

Circle the 🦆 if you hear /u/.

Put an X on 🦆 if you do not hear /u/.

Skills: Recognize the sound and symbol for short vowel /u/u.

Directions for how to make this phonics pull-through are on page 32.

ug

b d h j m r t

Skills: *Recognize the sound and symbol for short vowel /u/u; make words with short vowel u.*

How to Make a Phonics Pull-Through

1. Help your child cut out the picture of the ladybug and the initial consonant strip along the bottom of the page.
2. Cut slits on the ladybug along the dotted lines by folding your paper at a right angle to the lines and snipping.
3. Have your child turn the ladybug face down and thread the consonant strip through the slits. (Check to be sure the letters will be right side up when the pull-through fun begins!)
4. Tape the ends of the strip together to form a loop.

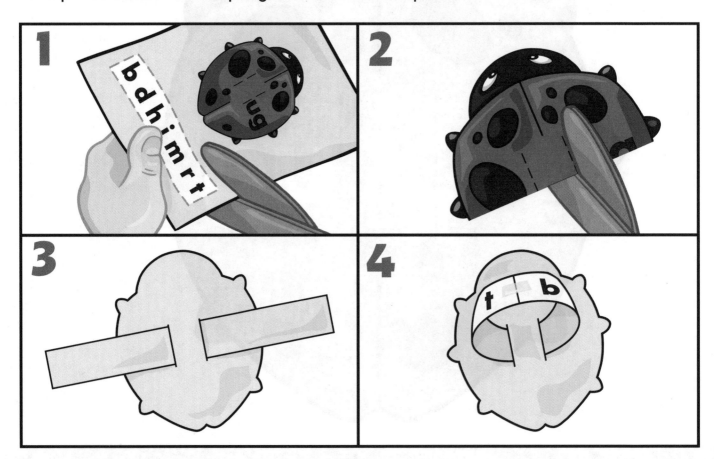

How to Use a Phonics Pull-Through

Have your child turn the ladybug over and pull the loop to show the first consonant. Ask your child to read the word: bug. Have your child keep pulling until each consonant letter is revealed and each word has been read.

You can make your own phonics pull-through to review any *group* of rhyming words you like!

SKILLS FOR

KINDERGARTEN

Teach your child—

- *to discriminate letter sounds and identify their symbols*
- *to understand a sequence of events*
- *to count sets and write the numbers 1 to 10*
- *to perform simple addition and subtraction*

About Skills For Kindergarten

Kindergarten is the first step in your child's formal education. While children develop at their own pace, most kindergarten teachers agree that five year olds can:

- identify most uppercase, but not lowercase, letters
- write some, but not all, letters of the alphabet
- read a few words
- make up rhyming words
- tell a story from a picture book
- write some numbers and tell their names
- draw most easy shapes
- count sets of up to 10 objects
- perform simple addition
- begin to understand money and how it is used

Teaching Kindergarten Skills At Home

You can help your child practice many of these important skills with materials you probably have right in your home:

- Use magnetic letters to focus on letter sounds. For example: show him or her the many words in the *–at* family—*bat*, *cat*, *fat*, and so on—and point out how only the beginning sound changes in each one.

- Read aloud from a favorite storybook, pausing before the last word or phrase on a page. Allow your child to complete it.

- When reading a new storybook, stop periodically and ask your child to predict what he or she thinks will happen next.

- Use simple household objects to build your child's skills in matching, sorting, sequencing, and counting.

- Use the kitchen for its endless opportunities to learn about math—numbers, sizes, measurements. For example: let your child help measure out ingredients as you make cookies.

Becoming Aware of Words and Numbers

It's easy to practice early reading and math skills with children—just help them become aware of how helpful words and numbers are in everyday life. For example:

- Point out important numbers to your child: his or her age, height, weight, address, or phone number.

- Count everyday items: napkins on a table, steps that lead to school, raisins in the trail mix.

- Look for numbers and words everywhere you go: on traffic signs, in advertisements, at the grocery store.

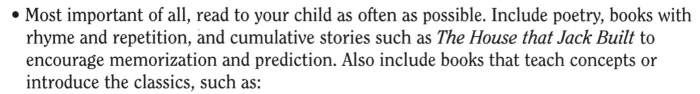

- Most important of all, read to your child as often as possible. Include poetry, books with rhyme and repetition, and cumulative stories such as *The House that Jack Built* to encourage memorization and prediction. Also include books that teach concepts or introduce the classics, such as:

  - *A Hatful of Seuss: Five Favorite Seuss Stories* by Dr. Seuss
  - *Have You Seen My Cat?* by Eric Carle
  - *Let's Count* by Tana Hoban

  - *Marvelous Math: A Book of Poems* by Lee Bennett Hopkins
  - *One Yellow Lion* by Martin Van Fleet
  - *Root-A-Toot-Toot* by Anne Rockwell

  - *The 20th Century Children's Book Treasury: Picture Books and Stories to Read Aloud* compiled by Janet Schulman

The material in this book is based on tried-and-true strategies that teachers use throughout this country. The Parents Magazine Tips and Hands-On Activities will help you incorporate kindergarten learning in a variety of activities that you and your child normally do throughout the day…and they'll help you make learning more fun! Remember that the ultimate goal of any instruction is not to teach isolated skills, but to impart strategies that children can use to learn throughout their lives.

Internet Resources for Parents

For articles and information about early learning and the stages of development of young children, check out these internet resources:

- Parents Magazine   http://www.parents.com

- Kid Source Online   http://www.kidsource.com

- Teaching Strategies, Inc.   http://www.teachingstrategies.com

- Learning Network Parent Channel   http://www.familyeducation.com

The Purr-fect Pet

Parents MAGAZINE **TIP** Identifying items that belong in a group helps children practice a skill called classification. This skill, which is important to all kinds of learning, can be easily practiced every day. The produce section of the supermarket, for example, offers many opportunities to classify by size, shape, color, and type.

A kitten makes a purr-fect pet!

Color all the pictures that belong in a pet store.

Skill: Identify items that belong in a group.

Let's build a doghouse.
Circle all the tools.
Put an **X** on all the things that **do not belong**.

Hands-On Activity

Tools for the Table
Have a pretend picnic and place assorted items at the center of the picnic blanket. Ask your child to help you set each place. Include items that belong, such as forks, spoons, plates, and napkins, as well as items that do not belong, such as miniature toys. As you sort through the items, ask what does and does not belong.

Skill: Identify items that belong in a group. 101

Funny Feet

A 🧦 and a 🧦 make a **pair**.
Circle the two pictures in each row
that make a **pair**.

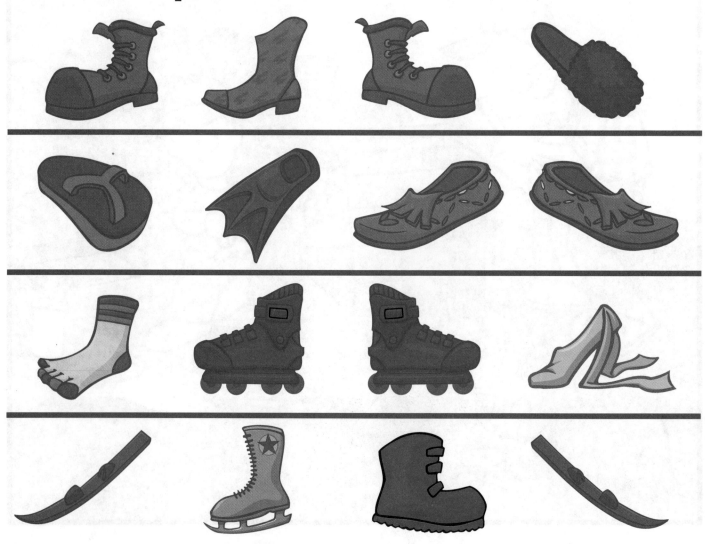

Skill: Use visual discrimination to identify matching pairs.

Help the little  get safely
to the bottom of the hill.
Draw a line from the to the .

Skill: Use fine motor skills to travel through a maze.

Same Sound Match Up

Say each picture name. Draw lines to match the pictures that begin with the same sound.

Skills: Recognize initial consonant sounds: /b/; /h/; /m/; /s/; /t/.

rhymes with .

They are a picture pair.
Find 3 more picture pairs
that rhyme. Circle each one.

Skill: Identify picture pairs that rhyme.

Eating Acorns

Parents MAGAZINE **TIP** As your child begins to form letters, point out the differences between letters that look alike. For b, d, p, and q, for example, point out the direction in which each letter is facing, which letters are "tall," and which ones "dip" below the line. For m, n, v, and w, explain that m has one more hump than n, and that w looks like two letter v's put together.

Draw a line from each uppercase letter to the matching lowercase letter.

Skill: Match uppercase and lowercase letters.

Fill in the missing letter.

A B C D E F G H I J K L M N O P Q R S T U V W X Y Z

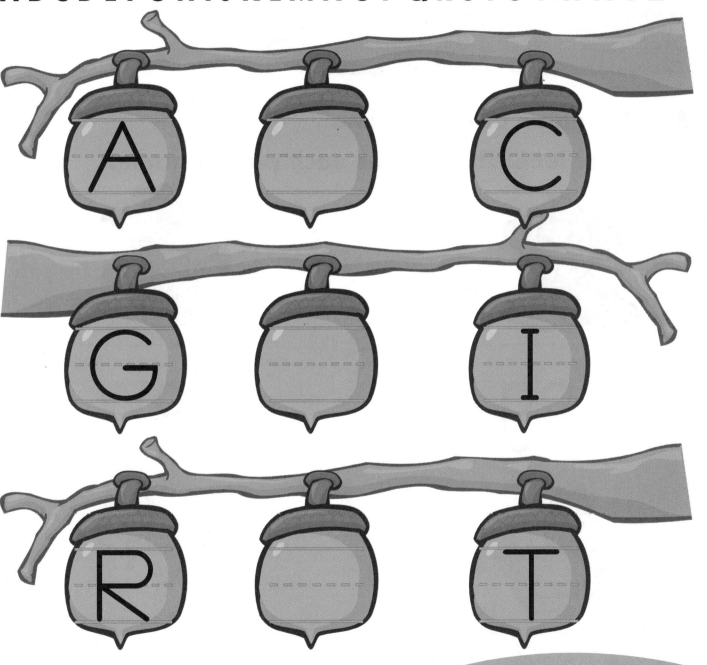

Skills: Write alphabet letters; complete a pattern of alphabet letters.

What Comes Next? **Hands-On Activity**
Use magnetic letters to create a sequence of three consecutive alphabet letters. Have your child continue the pattern by asking him or her to add the letter that comes next.

107

On the Farm

Parents MAGAZINE TIP Demonstrate how to blend sounds into words. Point to each picture on the page. Then say each sound in the word slowly, pointing to each letter as its sound is spoken. Stretch out the word dog, for example, and say dddoooggg. This technique will help your child learn how sounds go together to make words.

Say the name of each animal.

Write the letter that begins each picture name.

_____

og

_____

ow

_____

en

_____

oat

Skills: Recognize initial consonant sounds: /c/, /d/, /g/, /h/; write consonant letters: c, d, g, h.

Say the name of each animal.

Write the letter that completes each name.

ca

bu

fo

cu

Hands-On Activity

Sound Switch
Explain that you are going to play a word game. Ask your child to replace the first sound in each word you say with /s/. Then say **hand, bell, zip, rock, bun.** Try the activity with final sounds, using /p/, for example, and words such as **man, stem, hit, hog,** and **cut.**

The and ![boy face] and are having fun.

![girl] and ![boy] are **opposites.**

Draw lines between the words that are **opposites.**

Over

On

Off

Down

Under

Up

Skills: Identify opposites; match simple words and pictures.

Let's take a ride on a .

Color the spaces with **1 green**.
Color the spaces with **2 blue**.
Color the spaces with **3 red**.
Color the spaces with **4 brown**.
Color the spaces with **5 yellow**.

Hands-On Activity

Play It Safe! The playground is a great place to practice simple directions, as well as safety rules. Have your child follow simple one-step directions. For example, as he or she climbs the slide, say: Climb the ladder one step at a time. Once your child reaches the top of the slide, say: Sit down as soon as you get to the top.

Skills: Follow directions to complete a picture; use number and color words.

Schooltime Fun

The  and  have fun at school.

Write **1** to show what happened **first**.

Write **2** to show what happened **next**.

Write **3** to show what happened **last**.

Skill: Identify first, next, and last in a sequence of events.

Mama Clown is **bigger** than Baby Clown.

Baby Clown is **smaller** than Mama Clown.

Circle the one in each set that is **bigger**.

Send in the Clowns

Parents
MAGAZINE
TIP

Measuring objects is a great way to learn that the terms longer and shorter are all about comparisons. Choose an object to measure, such as a coffee table. Measure its length with a piece of string. Cut the string to the length of the table. Then challenge your child to use the string to find objects that are longer and shorter than the coffee table.

longer   **shorter**

Circle the one that is **longer** in each box.

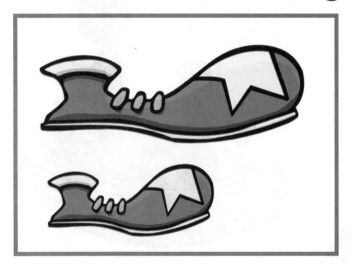

Skill: Identify objects that are longer.

Look at all these circus goodies!

Circle the set in each row that has more.

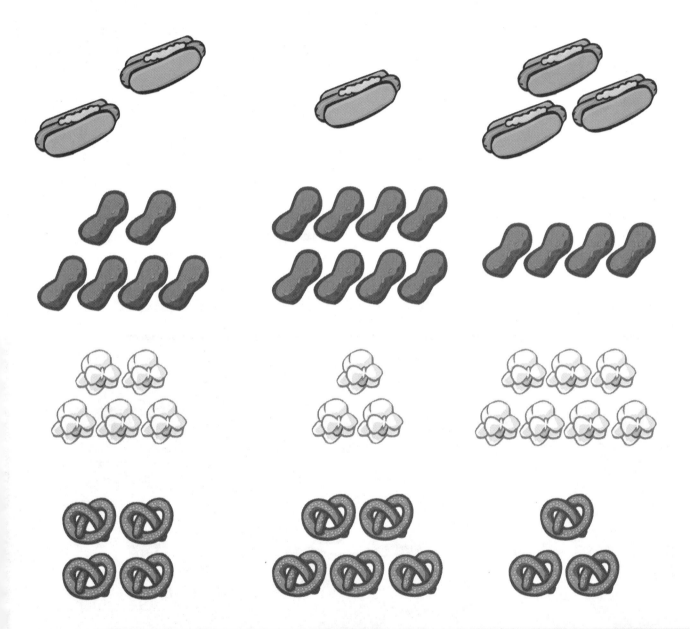

Skill: Identify sets that have more.

Backyard Fun

Shapes are everywhere! Have a shape hunt around the house or outdoors and look for round clocks, square windows, and triangular banners. Follow up by putting a square block in a bag with a round orange and a marble. Ask your child to touch and tell you which one doesn't belong.

Trace each shape.

circle

square

triangle

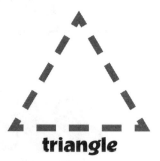 

rectangle

Find and circle each shape in the picture below.

Skills: Trace shapes (circle, square, rectangle, and triangle); identify shapes in a picture.

Funny Face

Make a funny face in this mirror!

Draw two little □s for eyes.

Draw a big △ nose.

Draw two ▭s for ears.

Draw a ○ for the mouth.

Add hair, a hat, and even a bow tie!

Hands-On Activity

Shape Placemats Provide your child with heavy paper in the size and shape of a placemat. Cut out different geometric shapes from colored paper and help your child glue the shapes around the placemat to form a pattern or design. Ask your child to identify each shape before it is glued onto the placemat. Then, together make a set of placemats for the whole family.

Give your funny face person a name.

Skills: Follow directions; use shapes to create a picture.   117

Say, I LOVE YOU!

Parents MAGAZINE **TIP** Ask your child to "read" the patterns on the page by saying for example, big red heart, small yellow heart, big red heart, small yellow heart, ___. Naming the sizes, colors, and shapes will help your child recognize the pattern in order to determine what comes next.

Here's one way to say, I LOVE YOU—
make a chain of paper hearts!
Draw and color the one that comes next.

Skills: Recognize a pattern of colors and sizes; continue a pattern.

Home, Sweet Home

Help each dog get back home.

Finish each path of colors and shapes.

Bugs in a Box

 **TIP** The activity on this page begins with the set, or group of objects, and asks your child to choose the corresponding number. Reinforc this skill in daily activities by beginning with the numeral and having your child create a set that represents it. For example, let your child use raisins, nuts, or any small item to make sets from 1 to 5.

How many bugs are in each box?
Circle the number that matches.

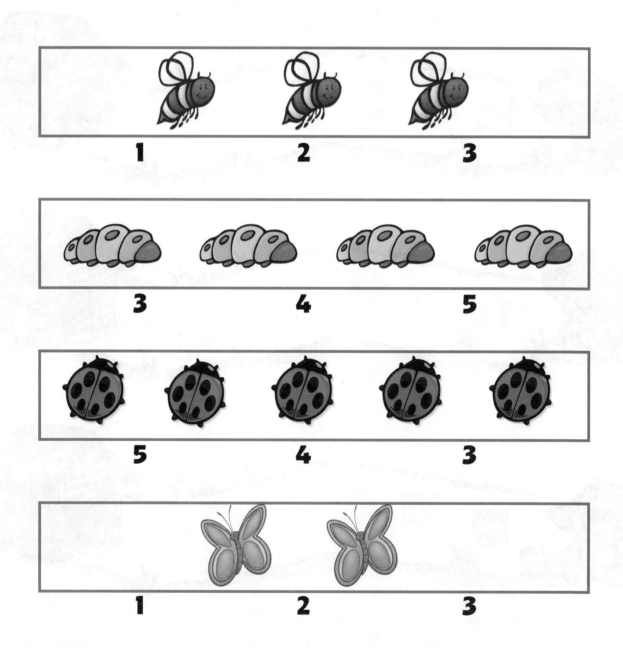

Skills: Count sets to 5; match sets to numerals.

Count each set. Draw a line to the correct number. Then trace and write the number.

Hands-On Activity

Number Rubbings
Place a piece of paper over your house numbers, a car's license plate, or any other raised numbers you can find. Take the wrapping off a crayon and rub with the crayon placed horizontally on top of the paper. As the pattern of numbers appears, have your child identify each numeral.

Skill: Count and write numerals 6 to 10.   121

All Aboard the Toy Train

Parents MAGAZINE **TIP** Math will mean so much more to your child if it is experienced in a personal way. Design a growth chart together and hang it on the wall. Mark the inches from 1 to 36. Let your child write in the first ten numerals on the chart, and then you write in the rest. The pattern of the numbers will soon become evident as your child observes his or her own charted growth.

The toy train is in town! Fill in the missing numbers.

1 _ 3

8 _ 10

5 _ 7

6 _ 8

7 _ 9

Skills: Write numerals; fill in missing numerals in sequence.

What takes you to toyland?
Connect the dots from 1 to 10.

Skill: Sequence the numerals 1 to 10.

How Many in All?

Parents MAGAZINE TIP

Explain to your child that add means to "put together." Model counting out sets, or groups, of small items and putting them together. Point to each item as you say: I have one. . . , two raisins. Now I add one more. I have one. . . , two. . . ,three raisins in all. Have your child repeat the process for counting out the sets for the equation 3 + 1 = 4.

Let's have a . Now let's have one more!
How many did we eat in all?

1   +   1   =   2

Add to find out how many in all.
Write the number on the line.

1   +   1   =    _____

2   +   1   =    _____

3   +   1   =   _____

4   +   1   =   _____

How Many Are Left?

Look at all these s.
Let's take away one.
How many are left?

Put an X on one in each group. Count how many are left.
Write the number on the line.

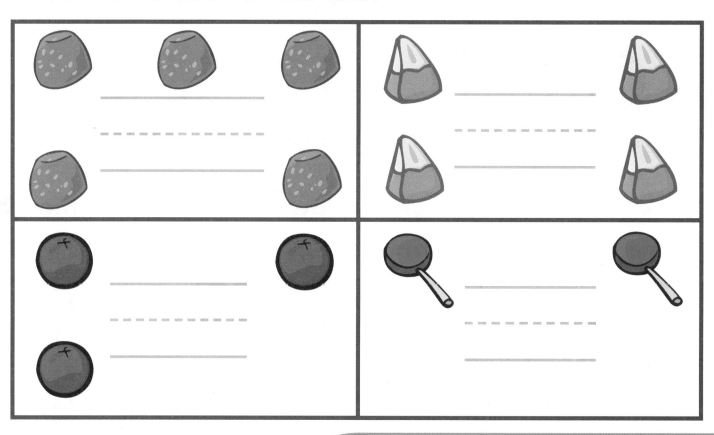

Skills: Do simple subtraction;
subtract 1 from sets.

Hands-On Activity

Pass the Basket!
Dinner is a great time to practice subtraction. For example, ask your child to help you count out the number of rolls in a bread basket. Then say: There are 5 rolls in the basket. I'm going to take one and put it on my plate. How many rolls will be left?

125

A Trip to the Piggy Bank

 **Since your child is just beginning to learn numbers and the value that each number represents, a good place to start building "money awareness" is with coins that reinforce counting from 1 to 10. Together, count out 10 pennies. Then, show your child equivalent values. For example: 5 pennies equal 1 nickel; 10 pennies equal 1 dime.**

Let's fill the piggy bank! This little piggy likes pennies, nickels, and dimes.

This is a penny.
A penny is one cent.

This is a nickel.
A nickel is five cents.

This is a dime.
A dime is ten cents.

Let's fill up the piggy bank. How many cents are there? Write the amount on the line.

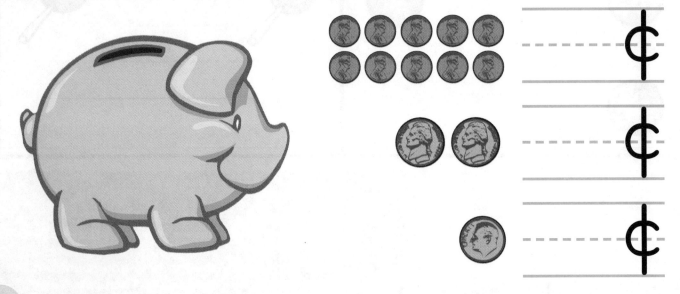

_____ ¢

_____ ¢

_____ ¢

Skill: Identify a penny, a nickel, and a dime.

Hands-On Activity

Penny Candy
Gather twenty cents in a variety of forms: 20 pennies, 4 nickels, and 2 dimes. Then, create a "pretend" store at home. Help your child count out 5 pennies in exchange for the "purchase" of a pretzel. Put a value on other items; then allow your child to "buy" them with the correct coins.

Count the money in each bank.
Draw a line to the correct amount.

   **10¢**

   **6¢**

   **20¢**

   **7¢**

Five Little Monkeys

Parents MAGAZINE TIP

This traditional counting rhyme is a great finger play. Practice with your child: Hold up five fingers for the five little monkeys. Place the fingers in the palm of your other hand to show the monkeys jumping. Hold up one finger to show the monkey that fell out of bed. Rub your head. Next, run your fingers across your other hand to show the monkeys running for the doctor. Finally, point and shake your finger as you repeat the doctor's warning.

Listen to this rhyme.
Then let's say it together!

Five little monkeys jumping on the bed.

One fell off and bumped his head.

They ran to the doctor and the doctor said, "No more monkeys jumping on the bed!"

Continue with four, three, two, and one monkey.

Skills: Learn a number chant; count down from 5 to 1.